Through a Widow's Window

&

Selected Poems

by Mary Elizabeth Lathers

Printed by CreateSpace, An Amazon.com Company
eStore address: www.CreateSpace.com/6898724

Most Scriptures taken from New King James Version
of the Holy Bible.

ISBN-10: 154283869X
ISBN-13: 978-1542838696

DEDICATION

This book is dedicated to my Lord and Savior, Jesus Christ, Who loved me and gave His life for me. Who also gave me an appreciation for poetry from early childhood. My prayer is that these poems will bring honor and glory to Him.

ACKNOWLEDGMENT

This book could never have been published without the long and tireless efforts of Chuck and Barbara Zonca. Chuck's skill in typing the poems and arranging the format has been invaluable. Both of their counsel, suggestions and encouragement have made the impossible possible, and the fruit of their labors has been a real joy for me. Thank you, dear friends, for being such a blessing to me in our mutual desire to serve and honor our Lord Jesus.

*"For from Him
and through Him
and to Him
are all things,
to Whom be glory
forever. Amen."*

Romans 11:36

PROLOGUE

I find much pleasure in writing poetry. But never did I plan to write poems about widowhood. The very thought of widowhood was depressing enough before my husband died on the very same day we were to bring him home from a hospital stay.

On that day the two words that first pierced my heart were, "He's gone!" I cannot describe my shock and grief, though a few of my poems make an attempt to do so. Only by God's amazing grace was I able to survive that day and the journey to follow.

I had never lived alone. David and I had been married fifty-four years. We had met at a summer session in Mexico while I was still in college. David had just obtained his Master's degree from the University of Michigan. After the session ended, we corresponded regularly, and two years later we were married.

Neither of us were true believers at the time, although we did attend church. A number of years later, I got saved at a Billy Graham Crusade. "Saved" was a word I neither knew nor understood because the churches we attended offered no gospel message and little Biblical truth; thus, they offered no hope through salvation and no assurance of salvation. Many years later, David, too, was saved.

A few years after my new birth, I became a diligent student of the Bible. I was absolutely amazed at its relevance to my everyday life. I yearned to know more and more about God and to have a closer relationship with Him. I learned the importance of knowing Scripture and applying it to all the areas of my life. Applying it was the most difficult part as I was strong-willed. But the Lord in His wisdom knew how to teach me many valuable lessons of surrender. Many I learned the hard way, but thanks to my Father's loving persistence, I did learn and I grew in grace and the knowledge of Him.

As Christians know, in the worst of circumstances, God frequently brings to remembrance a Scripture verse to rescue, guide, strengthen, comfort or sustain --- or all of the above. The Lord graciously supplied me with a verse very shortly after David's death. I had enjoyed this verse previously, and the Lord retrieved it from my past to use it for my present trial as a personal and comforting word from Him. It is Romans 11:36: "For <u>from</u> Him, and <u>through</u> Him, and <u>to</u> Him, are all things: to Whom be glory forever." This verse is literally written in stone now --- on our tombstone.

The Lord made it very clear that David was a gift <u>from</u> Him. God Himself ordained our meeting in Mexico. We were not from the same state, and graduation and a career were my only goals, not marriage. So, we had an arranged marriage, an arrangement <u>from</u> God.

<u>Through</u> Him we were married many long and blessed years. <u>Through</u> Him we became parents of two wonderful sons, among countless other blessings. <u>Through</u> Him we both received the greatest of all gifts, our salvation.

Then, "<u>to</u> Him." God took David <u>to</u> Him, <u>to</u> His heavenly home. Though death is a great loss for loved ones left on earth, going <u>to</u> Him is the best of all of life's journey because it is followed by eternal joy and peace with our Creator Who redeemed us with His blood.

Time passed slowly after David's death, and as the Lord was in the process of healing me, I began writing poems about widowhood. A friend had given me a prose book on this subject, and I found the author's shared experiences helpful. Might not a poetry book also be helpful and comforting to others? The Lord confirmed to me the need to share my thoughts and experiences in verse.

As I compiled some poems for widows, the Lord strongly prompted me to include many other selected poems on various subjects for those who may not be widows but simply enjoy poetry. Also, the book might be an encouragement to those longing for life and light and truth in a world that is dark and cruel and senseless.

My prayer for the reader is this: That all readers who have experienced the death of a spouse will be strengthened and comforted. But also, that all readers who have not received Jesus' free gift of salvation will do so, both through the messages of the poems and through the truth of the Scriptures, the very words of life, contained on these pages.

CONTENTS

Seasons Of Widowhood

"He changes the times and the seasons." Daniel 2:21

Through My Autumn Window

I lost him in midsummer
When sky was blue
And grass was green.
Now has burst upon me
A very different scene.
Outside my autumn window
Riotous colors glare
And with bravado of their brilliance
Their dominance declare.
Beauty, color everywhere!
Yet dying and death are all around
As withered stalks stand stark and brown.
As shriveled leaves float to autumn ground.
You, Lord, designed this awesome change.
Weather, earth, sky, You rearrange,
But for me this season seems odd, seems strange.
Lord, grant me trust to bring me through.
I look nowhere else.
I look to You
In all that You change.
In all that You do.
Out of season's loss bring gain.
Let my love for You never wane.
Though seasons come
And seasons go,
Let my trust in You
Be never so.

"In God I will praise His Word,
in God I have put my trust..."
Psalm 56:4

"Trust in the LORD with all your heart, and lean not on your
own understanding; in all your ways acknowledge Him, and
He shall direct your paths." Proverbs 3:5-6

Through My Winter Window

*D*rooping boughs downward bend
From tall, snow-laden pines.
An exquisite beauty to winter season
God has graciously assigned.
Heaps of fluffy, snowy mounds
Crown shrunken rail and fencepost
And blanket frozen ground.
The icy creek is barely flowing.
The icy wind has ceased its blowing.
Silence comforts as silence surrounds.
From morning until evening
Until the day's demise,
Snowflakes soft
Slowly, lazily waft
From graying winter skies.
The hours pass slowly; dusk advances.
The tranquil view my peace enhances.
God's peace. So gentle, so amazing.
He lends contentment
Through my windowgazing.
Rejoicing at nature's loveliness,
I cannot cease from praising.
Long winter, lonely winter.
Dark days to come, austere.
Yet winter of many blessings
A winter of drawing near.

"Draw near to God and
He will draw near to you."
James 4:8

4

Through My Spring Window

Warm, pleasant rays of an early spring sun
Slant through my window, beam across my room.
Winter has departed, a new season has begun.
Buds, flowers, blossoms, all blissful in their bloom.

Bright forsythia flaunts its golden sprays.
The view from my window is a lovely, welcome scene.
Chartreuses and emeralds mingle in exuberant display.
Delightful is my landscape of green upon green.

When my gaze becomes misted with momentary sadness,
I see beyond a transient spring and a sky of transient blue.
I rejoice in an approaching season, one of eternal gladness
In the presence of my Savior---and with my loved one, too.

"For lo, the winter is past,
The rain is over and gone.
The flowers appear on the earth"
Song of Solomon 2:11-12

Through My Summer Window

A year this summer.
Again it is July.
Day by day by day,
The weeks, the months
Have travelled by.
A year has passed
Full circle
Since he has passed away.
Today,
From my window
A bright display
Of iridescent green.
An old, familiar
Summer scene.
Flowers, ferns
Creeping vines
Bask cheerfully under
A sun that shines
And intrudes into my room.
And, yes, in part,
Into my heart.
Dispelling a touch of gloom.
I ponder now
A year of grace.
Immeasurable grace.
Grace to cover
And to fill
So much pervasive quietness,
So much solemn still!

A year of uninvited space
And ever, ever slower pace.
Lord, You are so gracious.
Lord, You are so good.
No human, earthly counsel,
No fortitudinous trying
Ever would
Or ever could
Cease my inward crying,
Or ease the pain.
Or imbue with strength,
Your divine
And cherished gain.
Nothing, nothing
Can take the place
Of Your abundant grace.
All praise is due,
Dear Lord, to You.
In all these seasons
You have been faithful.
You have proven true.
Now, dear Lord,
The first long year
Has passed.
Now brighter hope
I hold
With ever tighter grasp.

"This hope we have as an anchor of the soul."
Hebrews 6:19

Through a Later Window

*T*oday two years have come and gone.
Each day brings strength through Christ alone.
Each day new grace at each new dawn.
Each night sweet sleep when day is done.

Each day some sadness, yet far less weeping.
My Savior my soul is ever keeping.
My thoughts toward heaven more often leaping,
My trust in the Lord He's daily deepening.

I've so many promises on which to stand,
So many touches from His merciful hand.
Now, a wider perspective of His infinite plan,
And more peace on the journey to the Promised Land.

Lord, there is work to do before night arrives.
Let me be used by You in others' lives.
Grant me someone to lead and by Your gospel guide
To the Savior Who loves them to walk by His side.

*Jesus said, "I must work the works of Him who sent Me
while it is day; the night is coming when no one can work."*
John 9:4

*"For I am not ashamed of the gospel of Christ, for it is the
power of God to salvation for everyone who believes..."*
Romans 1:16

Widows Of The Bible

The Widow of Zarephath
(An Old Testament Widow)

*E*lijah, God's faithful prophet, once by ravens fed,
Went to the city of Zarephath, by the good Lord clearly led.
There he met an impoverished widow; her straits were very dire.
Her life was slowly ebbing as she gathered sticks for a fire.
A famine had stricken each family in that parched and dusty land,
But awaiting her were miracles from God's Almighty hand.
Elijah requested of the widow some water and a morsel of bread.
"I have but a handful of flour and a bit of oil," she said.
She was preparing these meager staples when Elijah happened by,
For herself and for her son to eat. Soon of hunger they would die.
Elijah told her not to fear but to proceed her meal to bake,
And from her scanty recipe to bring him first a cake.
He promised supply of flour and oil. There would be no longer dearth.
The Lord, then, at a later time, would send rain upon the earth.
She did as he said, and Elijah, for a time, with the widow resided,
And for many days both the oil and flour were graciously provided.
But when the widow's little son was later stricken ill,
She asked, "Did you come to remember my sin and then my son to kill?"
Elijah told her to bring the boy to the upper room where he stayed.
And there on his bed he laid him and to God he fervently prayed.
As he stretched himself upon the boy, he prayed and also cried
For the little lad's soul to return to him, and the Lord the child revived!
Elijah took him to his mother, and she saw the amazing proof
That Elijah was a man of God, and the words he spoke were truth.
God sent his prophet to a widow in a parched and pagan nation.
She needed food. She needed her son. Most of all she needed salvation.
God watches over widows. He knows their every want and need.
Whatever her situation, the widow blessed with salvation is a widow blessed indeed.

I Kings 17:8-24

11

Elisha and the Widow
(An Old Testament Miracle)

A widow whose husband had feared the Lord
Was desperate as creditors appeared at her door.
She cried out to Elisha of her plight, of her spouse.
She had nothing but a vessel of oil in her house.

Elisha had her borrow empty jars from her neighbors.
Then he instructed her how to perform her labors.
She and her sons must first shut the door,
Then from her one jar into the empty ones pour.

She kept pouring the oil; no empty vessel remained.
Then she reported to the prophet her miraculous gain.
He told her to sell the oil and pay off her debt.
Then she and her sons could live off the rest.

How blessed this widow. How blessed her sons.
They would always remember what God had done.
Every widow o'er the ages who has trusted in the Lord
Has found Him ever faithful. He will always keep His word.

2 Kings 4:1-7

*"A father of the fatherless, a defender of widows,
is God in His holy habitation." Psalm 68:5*

Ruth - A Story of Two
Old Testament Widows

*N*aomi lost Elimelech, her beloved husband and friend.
Then, sadly, two sons followed him to a far too early grave.
Indescribable Naomi's sorrow; her mourning saw no end.
But God provided her with Ruth, trusting, loyal, brave.

The Lord provided protection for the journey to Naomi's home.
Across long and weary and arid miles Ruth and Naomi trod.
God had a glorious plan for them, these two widows all alone.
Oh, it was a great and awesome plan from a gracious sovereign God.

God was their faithful provider as they settled in Canaan land.
There Ruth was divinely sent to glean in Boaz's fields of wheat.
God raised up a Kinsman Redeemer, a godly Hebrew man,
And Ruth would find favor in his eyes the moment they would meet.

When her Kinsman Redeemer and Ruth were wed, what a joy to the family came!
Theirs a story of hope and redemption for all who read its pages.
From their lineage came The Redeemer, Jesus, name above all names.
Out of the grief of two helpless widows, God brought Life to all the ages.

Book of Ruth

The Widow of Nain
(A New Testament Widow)

*T*here was a small city in Galilee
Near Nazareth called Nain.
When Jesus and the disciples entered it,
Near the gate was a woman in pain.
A dead man was being carried out,
The beloved only son of his mother.
She had suffered long her husband's loss,
And now the tragic death of another.
A crowd from the city followed her,
Some in sorrow and mourning deep,
But the Lord on the widow had compassion
And said to her, "Do not weep."
He came and touched the open coffin.
Death the deceased could no longer keep.
His words to the man were simply,
"I say to you arise."
And he who was dead obeyed and arose
To the incredulous crowd's surprise.
Jesus presented him to his mother;
All knew a great prophet had come.
A great miracle all for the glory of God,
A widow received back her son!
Jesus ever cares for the widow.
He sees her tears and hears her sighs.
He speaks to each widow who follows Him
Let Your faith arise.

Luke 7:11-16

Reflections On Widowhood

His Word, My Strength

*D*ying, then death, then a widow's plunge to grief.
First the process of losing, then the agony of loss.
Will time ever heal? Bring one moment of relief?
Yes, Jesus is the healer, He Who died on the cross.

The process. Then reality. Then finality to face.
Gone! Indescribable the heft of that brief word.
It pierces the heart. Would seem to cancel grace
But for the merciful help and comfort of the Lord.

Loneliness engulfs. Its waves relentless pound.
Each day brings a new and unique flood of sorrow.
Then a Word from the Lord. a sweet, strengthening sound.
A verse long forgotten brings solace for the morrow.

"From Him, through Him, to Him are all things."
God, the giver of marriage, gave for an appointed time.
He's sovereign in my onward journey toward Him my Lord and King,
And through His strength alone I'll follow His calendar divine.

*"For of Him and through Him
and to Him are all things."
Romans 11:36*
(This is the first of many Scriptures
that sustained me through
the first year of widowhood.)

Death Came Knocking

*D*eath came knocking
At my door.
I opened to see it
Standing there.
A loved one gone.
Though much my pain,
It was something
I could bear.

Death came knocking
At my door.
I opened it to face
Death's cruelest stare.
My husband gone.
I could not endure,
That is sure,
Were it not for
Jesus' presence there.

Jesus said,
"I will never leave you
nor forsake you."
Hebrews 13:5

Widowhood

*W*hen widowhood comes,
At first it numbs.
It numbs with disbelief.
But then it goes
Into the throes
Of stabbing, piercing grief.
Relentless
Its stress
Of hopelessness.

But grace is there
In our deepest despair.
Our loving Lord
Does see,
Does care.
Do heed His promises
So precious, so warming.
Joy <u>will</u> come
Some
Future morning.

"Weeping may endure for a night,
But joy comes in the morning."
Psalm 30:5

My Times Are in Your Hand

$\mathcal{L}$ord, my times are in Your hand.
All the days and years. All of my life.
It was foreordained in Your sovereign plan
The moment I would cease to be a wife.

Lord, my times are in Your hand.
Long we kept our vow, "Until death do us part."
Then in Your sovereign, omniscient plan,
You ceased the beating of my loved one's heart.

Lord, my times are in Your hand.
Were his death later, would grief be less?
You number our days in Your eternal plan.
Help me to embrace it and trust You to bless.

Lord, my times are in Your hand.
All flesh is as grass that soon fades away.
Sorrowing and rejoicing are both in Your plan,
And, oh, the rejoicing at heaven's meeting one day.

"My times are in Your hand..."
Psalm 31:15

Psalm 139

New Widow

I often wonder how my Lord sustains me
As He keeps me running this earthly race.
How does He keep me moving forward
When so often I choose to run in place?

Is it by His grace or His great mercy?
Or is it all by His redeeming love?
Is it, perhaps, by the Word of His power?
The answer? By all of the above.

"... being confident
of this very thing,
that He Who has begun
a good work in you
will complete it
until the day
of Jesus Christ..."
Philippians 1:6

Everlasting Love

God's love for me is everlasting.
It will never diminish, never increase.
In time of grief, in time of testing,
It's the thought of His love that brings me peace.

God's love for me is so wide and deep.
I've never a worry it will ever cease.
When the path ahead winds crooked and steep,
It's the thought of His love that brings me peace.

God's love for me has brought me salvation.
It broke my chains --- what blessed release!
Now in Christ I am a new creation.
It's the thought of His love that brings me peace.

God's love for me is all sustaining
With Christ as my Counselor and Great High Priest.
When there are no more days for me remaining,
I'll dwell eternally in His love and peace.

"For God so loved the world
that He gave His only begotten Son,
that whoever believes in Him
should not perish
but have everlasting life."
John 3:16

We Were Wives

We were wives.
Busily doing what good wives do.
We were friends
And lovers
And helpmeets
And caregivers
And mothers.
Busy with our lives,
It was all that we knew.

Now we are widows.
The days seem long
With no more wifely things to do.
Still,
We are mothers
And prayer warriors
And friends
And counselors
And neighbors.
As servants of the living God
Lord, use these years
To serve and glorify You.

Our Sons

His children meant the world to him.
They made his heart both proud and glad.
He desired always the best for them.
He was there for them in good times and bad.

As I saw my sons' grief at their father's death,
It added sorrow upon sorrow to me.
Yet, observing their love, its depth and breadth,
Was a blessing and a beautiful thing to see.

Our Home

*O*ur home. My, how it has grown!
No longer ours, now simply my own.
Larger now, and the rooms less cheerful.
Filled with memories fond and often tearful.

Some widows move to other dwellings.
But I dread the thought of ever selling.
Some find it easier to begin anew.
But for me, no other house will do.

He chose the plan. He chose the lot.
For fifty-plus years our togetherness spot.
He loved the house, the creek, the grounds.
He built the picket fence that surrounds.

Lord, You provided for us this special space.
I am so very grateful. I desire no other place.
But there is an exception: our home in glory above
That he and I will share together in Your eternal love.

"And I will dwell in the house
of the LORD forever."
Psalm 23:6

A Widow's End of Day

My day is done
Without the one
With whom I spent
Each ending.
My day is done
Until the sun
Rises
Bright, befriending.

My day is done
But soon will come
A day that closes
Never.
Spent with the Son,
With my departed one,
The three of us
Together!

*"Christ the firstfruits, afterward those
who are Christ's at His coming."
1 Corinthians 15:23*

A Widow's Strength

*F*rom strength to strength
I climb
Yet more steepening path of time.
From strength to strength I dare
More difficult ascending stair.
From strength to strength
I step
Through unexplored,
Unmeasured depth.
From strength to strength
I tread
Where never before
Was ever led.
From strength to strength
I forward move
By grace upheld
In Jesus' love.
From strength to strength
Toward heaven's gate,
And there no need
For strength awaits.

"They go from strength to strength;
Each one appears before God in Zion."
Psalm 84:7

There's a Silence

There's a silence that blesses on a cold winter day.
There's a hush solemn but peaceful in nature's display.
Snow on field, on woodland in soft, heaping mound.
How awesome the serenity of never a sound!

There's the silence of sunset at decline of the day.
The silence of the sky in brilliance arrayed.
There's a welcome tranquility in twilight dim.
Sun's farewell splendor on horizon's red rim.

Silence, I've learned, oft' with loneliness blends.
But silence, I've learned, is often a friend.
Lord, in these silent years in whatever I do,
Use this abundance of silence to glorify You.

"Give to the Lord the glory due His name."
1 Chronicles 16:29

On Silence

*S*ilence can seem so welcome,
Like a sweet, endearing friend.
But silence can be all invasive,
Inviting itself to end.

Silence can be such a blessing
As it permeates the room,
Or it can hover depressing,
Encompassing like a tomb.

Silence, be it shunned or welcomed,
In my life has taken much space.
I am growing more now to enjoy it
And to embrace it by God's grace.

"Be still, and know that I am God."
Psalm 46:10

"In quietness and confidence
shall be your strength."
Isaiah 30:15

A Widow to Her Soul

*B*less the Lord
O my soul!
All that is within me
Bless His holy name.
Bless the Lord
O my soul!
Bless Him in the knowing
That life will never be the same.

Bless the Lord
O my soul!
Though you feel no desire
To bless.
Bless Him still
And thank Him still
In your time
Of deep distress.

Bless the Lord
O my soul!
Let His benefits
Be forgotten not.
Remember His
Precious promises,
The truths that
He has taught.

Bless the Lord
O my soul!
Seek His wider,
Grander view.
Soon you will
Behold Him.
He is ever faithful.
He is ever true.

Bless the Lord
O my soul!
He is blessing you
In your sorrow.
He will never leave you
Nor forsake you.
Trust Him now, today,
Trust Him each tomorrow.

Psalm 103

A Widow's Plea for Guidance

You have established
Your throne in heaven.
Your Kingdom, Lord,
Rules over all.
Rule over me, Lord,
In each decision I make,
Though the matter
Be ever so small.

You are sovereign over
Your people, Lord.
I do seek to know
Your will for me.
As I face this strange
New season of life,
Give me ears to hear.
Give me eyes to see.

I look back upon
Our married years.
Upon all Your guidance
So graciously given.
Much more now, Lord,
I need to be guided
By the all-wise God.
I need to hear from heaven.

Help me as I come
Before Your throne.
Though my prayer be long
Or but a minute.
Let me hear your voice
And Yours alone.
Let me hear You say,
"This is the way.
Walk ye in it!"

"Your ears shall hear a word behind you,
saying, 'This is the way, walk in it,'
Whenever you turn to the right hand
Or whenever you turn to the left."
Isaiah 30:21

"Your word is a lamp to my feet
And a light to my path."
Psalm 119:105

Strong in the Lord

Be strong in the Lord, dear widow.
Be strong in the power of His might.
Be strong in the lonely days ahead,
In the long, solemn hours of the night.

Be strong. Be strong and courageous.
This is the Lord's repeated command.
Be strengthened with might through His Spirit.
Grow strong in your inner man.

God knows of your need and your weakness.
He'll provide you His strength to stand.
He sees the plight of every widow.
He'll uphold you with His mighty right hand.

*"That He would grant you, according to the riches
of His glory, to be strengthened with might
through His Spirit in the inner man."*
Ephesians 3:16

*"He gives power to the weak,
And to those who have no might
He increases strength."*
Isaiah 40:29

34

Nature

Green

$\mathcal{T}$he green of the trees, the bushes, the grass.
There is no color that can ever surpass
The shimmering, radiant, sun-kissed hue
Of green of spring drenched with morning dew.

The green of the evergreens in tall heights ranging
In varying shades. In winter unchanging.
In autumn a backdrop to landscapes supreme.
Russets, gold, crimsons against remnants of green.

Spring brings its welcome with green, grassy floor.
Expanses of lawn surround gardens' decor.
A summery delight are mossy meadows serene,
And God's playgrounds for children He painted all green.

I've wondered quite often, What if things were reversed?
What if sky were deep green over God's blue earth?
But the all-wise Painter chose the perfect color scheme.
Thank You, dear Lord, for Your bountiful green.

I Will Lift My Eyes to the Hills

I never more
Significant am
Nor less,
Than when, Dear Lord,
You bless --- and bless---
Me to survey
On cloudless-clear,
Or soft and misty day
Your lofty peaks.
Your layered ranges
Rise first to point
And then to shriek
Both to sky
And all who espy
That you are Creator.
Omnipotence speaks
As your majestic peaks
Shout, "Glorify!"
And, as I,
Here at mountains' feet
Behold where meet
Sky and peak,
Nothing, no one else
I seek.

I lift up my eyes
Unto the hills,
To You Who reign
Over every mountain,
Valley, plain.
And, oh, the wonder
Oh, the thrill
That You, Creator
Of these hills
Rule and reign
In majesty above
Over all beneath
And all around.
Over me with love!
Me! Mere speck
Upon Your ground.
I gaze in awe
Where mountains tower
And rest secure
In Your
Great sovereignty and power.
Oh, Lord of splendor,
Love and grace,
Keep me in this mountain place.

Psalm 121

Birdsound

I heard the cawing of a crow,
A most distracting sound.
Its repetition was annoying
As it kept circling over the ground.

I heard the crowing of a rooster.
Cheerful. But its long encore
Reminds of that historic moment
When Peter wept before the Lord.

I heard the strident call of the bluejay.
Beautifully plumed, this bird did not cease
To dominate the neighborhood.
It was not prone to keep the peace.

I heard the sweet chirping of a junco.
Its song a welcome, uplifting word.
So endearing that tiny, drab, humble creature,
God's most understated bird.

Psalm 148

One Bird

*O*ne bird singing
On a gray March morning.
One bird perched
On a limb of a tree.
One bird outpouring
A lilting aria.
One bird singing
Especially to me.

One bird's trilling
Filling air with sweet song.
One bird's warbling
Composed by Sovereignty.
One bird's purest music
In a world gone so wrong.
One bird's melody
Sending happiness to me.

One bird bringing
Glory to the Father.
One bird fulfilling
All it was created to be.
One little bird's joyful solo
Spreading hope and comfort.
One bird teaching
Many lessons to me.

"All Your works shall praise You, O LORD*..."*
Psalm 145:10

The Leaf

A bright crimson leaf,
A lovely maple leaf.
Perfect in form,
Of flawless complexion.
Waiting for me
Beneath an autumn tree.
Lovelier still
At closer inspection.
The fairest of all
My leaf collection.
Yet in the midst
Of my admiring gladness.
I felt for a moment
A touch of sadness.
The beauty of my
Cherished leaf
Would soon be gone,
Its charm quite brief.

Soon it would be
Faded and curled.
Gone the way
Of this dying world.
Then I remembered
With thought less sober,
That sunlit day
In mid-October,
This briefness is all
By God's design.
And for those of us
Past our prime,
Unlike a leaf,
Faded and dry,
Merely fluttering by,
We can still
Bring Him glory
Before we die.

"Give to the LORD the glory due His name..."
1 Chronicles 16:29

A Lone Daisy

A daisy in mid-November bloomed.
Among fallen leaves it graced my yard.
Alone it stood with cheerful face
And endured dark nights both cold and hard.

Lord, like that lone daisy I need to grow.
In this dark and fallen world, I need firm to stand.
I want others to see You, desire so many to know
The One Who upholds me with His righteous right hand.

"Fear not, for I am with you;
Be not dismayed,
For I am your God.
I will strengthen you,
Yes, I will help you,
I will uphold you with
My righteous right hand."
        Isaiah 41:10

Savoring His Beauty

*W*hen I am surrounded by a soft, gray mist,
I am filled with peace, with a subtle bliss.
When I observe the brilliant descending sun,
My sinful pride is all undone.
When I walk in a gentle summer rain,
It is hard to focus on petty pain.
When I gaze upon stars in their galaxies,
Earthly amusements hold no interest for me.
When I behold the beauty of an indigo sky,
Then foolish endeavors cannot satisfy.
When I behold the majesty of a mountain peak,
No other thrill do I want nor do I seek.
When I tread the sands of the ocean shore,
I desire nothing else. I want no more.
When I hear thundering roar of a waterfall,
No other music can my ear recall.
When I survey a meadow of sunflowers bright,
My heart fills with joy. I gasp with delight.
When I view cliffs poised above foam-frothed waves,
I'm enthralled in a moment I wish forever to save.
When I explore forest paths beneath redwood trees,
How insignificant are man's achievements to me.
When I observe the sliver of a crescent moon,
I so yearn for its Creator to come back soon.
Then, all this exquisite beauty, seemingly unsurpassed,
Will be replaced with His glory that forever will last.

"O LORD, how manifold are Your works!
In wisdom You have made them all.
The earth is full of Your possessions---"
Psalm 104:24

Summer Evening Rain

There is a wonderful winsomeness
And a lingering pleasantness
About a summer evening rain
As it splatters on lawn and windowpane.
It arrives as a welcome descending dew
Relieving the scorching heat of day,
Washing its layers of dust away,
While lending sweet music of splashing drops, too.
Its fragrance rivals that of all the flowers
As it permeates the air of the evening hour.
Summer rain. God's gift, a blessed delight,
As it cools and refreshes the long summer night.

"Every good gift and every perfect gift
is from above, and comes down
from the Father of lights,
with Whom there is no variation
or shadow of turning."
James 1:17

Life's Greatest Contrast

*B*lack trunks of trees,
Dark gray sky.
Fields somber, brown.
Then surprise, delight
At winter's first sight
Of contrast in white.
The white of snowflakes
Tumbling down.
All life is contrast.
Creation makes it clear.
The weather, nature, color,
The seasons of the year.
How shall we then live
With such surrounding proof?
Shall we not love our Creator?
Love His enduring truth?
Or, shall we,
In contrast,
Live in the black of sin
With neither His Light
Nor life within?
In darkness live,
In darkness die,
Choosing to believe
Not God's Truth,
But Satan's lie?

"Then Jesus spoke ... saying, "I am the light of the world. He who follows Me shall not walk in darkness, but have the light of life." John 8:12

Winds of Life

The summer zephyr
Ever softly blows
Bestowing fresh coolness
As it lightly passes.
It rustles not
But whispers low
As it ripples through
The meadow grasses.

The March wind whistles;
It harshly blows.
A bitter, relentless
Chill it brings.
A last hurrah,
As if it knows
It soon must yield
To warmth of Spring.

The winter wind howls;
Its blasts are fierce.
It preys on all,
All nature surrounds.
Its gusts are tireless;
They stab, they pierce.
All seek shelter from
Its cold and sound.

"The wind blows
Where it wishes,"
Jesus once said.
"You can't tell where it
Comes from
Or where it goes."
But those born of the Spirit
Their Savior know,
And by His Spirit
They are led.

*"The wind blows where it wishes, and you hear the
sound of it, but cannot tell where it comes from
and where it goes. So is everyone who is born
of the Spirit." John 3:8*

*Jesus answered and said to him (Nicodemus),
"Most assuredly, I say to you, unless one is born
again, he cannot see the kingdom of God."
John 3:3*

Silhouettes on a Hill

*B*lack trees towering on a distant hill.
Above a winter landscape set.
Tall and straight their silhouette
Against a rose-tinged morning sky.
   Trees: Striking in their contrast,
      Fascinating to the eye.

An aging farmhouse set high on a hill
With fresh-mown pastures that surround.
Sun reflecting through weathered windowpanes
As it descends so slowly down.
   A house: Silhouetted against an evening sky.
      A lonesome sight to the passerby.

Black cattle silhouetted on a distant hill.
Below, rural farmlands all around.
An ancient barn leaning, a rustic old mill.
A wagon heading toward a distant town.
   Cattle: Peacefully grazing in green of May
      Enjoying the sun of a late spring day.

A tall wooden cross on Calvary's hill.
Most significant of all earth's dark silhouettes.
Set stark against history, it all history fills,
A place that man will never forget.
   A cross: Bleak against Israel's darkening skies
      There the Savior died --- only to rise.

Jesus said ..."I am the resurrection and the life.
He who believes in Me, though he may die, he shall live."
John 11:25

Praises, Prayers
and Ponderings

He Cares For You

Praise to our **H**oly God.
Praise to our **E**ternal God.

Praise to our **C**reator God.
Praise to our **A**lmighty God.
Praise to our **R**ighteous God.
Praise to our **E**verlasting God.
Praise to our **S**overeign God.

Praise to our **F**aithful God.
Praise to our **O**mnipotent God.
Praise to our **R**edeemer God.

Praise to our **Y**ahweh God.
Praise to our **O**mniscient God.
Praise to our **U**nfailing God.

"Trust in the Lord with all your heart."
Proverbs 3:5

"Cast all your cares on Him because
He cares for you."
1 Peter 5:7

One Book Only

*P*salm strength,
Gospel grace,
Epistle's clear direction.
Let there be no drifting from this place
Of God's divine protection.

Jesus' life.
The prophets' call.
The lessons learned of kings.
Let there be no compromise at all
Of Truth's eternal things.

Precepts ---
His firm commands.
Proverbs' counsel wise.
Let there be ears to hear what God demands
Of consecrated lives.

One Book.
And only one
Sustaining this perilous age.
Let there be the preeminence of God's Perfect Son
Through the power of each page.

Psalm 119

His Lovingkindness

His mercy endures forever.
Forever!
The words of the psalm
Repeat.
Reverberate. So
That we never underestimate
The compassion of our God.
His mercy means lovingkindness.
Not that God is mindless
Of our sin.
It's His very mercy,
(Along with His grace)
That causes us to face,
As we look within,
All that displeases Him.
'Tis His mercy
Compels us to hate
What His holiness
Will judge,
Not tolerate.

→

By mercy His Spirit
Is sent
To break our evil pride,
Put self and selfishness
Aside
And repent.
And believe!
And yet more mercy receive!
How can we, dear Lord,
Ever enough appreciate
Your love so great?
The words of Your psalm,
A balm,
As they reverberate.

Psalm 118

Our Stability

*G*od is the stability of our times
When all the world in darkness gropes.
When evil forces strong aligned
Oppose the Lord of light and hope.

God is the stability of our times
When pleasure, wealth, success allure
The thoughts of mortal, carnal minds
From truth that's absolute and pure.

God is the stability of our times
When technology struts across the stage,
While philosophies play their role divine
And God watches as the heathen rage.

God is the stability of our times
When religion offers many gates
Broad and beckoning. Enticing climes
Which Satan opens --- then awaits.

God is the stability of our times
When madness grips the small and great,
And no discernment of His signs
Reminds the soul the hour is late.

God is the stability of our times
When deception has the final say
Over multitudes who will decline
That Jesus is the only Way.

$\rightarrow$

God is the stability of our times.
For such a time as this, His the sovereign plan.
I'll not leave you nor forsake you, His promise reminds.
"I'll forever uphold you by My righteous right hand."

For He (God) Himself has said,
"I will never leave you nor forsake you."
Hebrews 13:5

I Want To Do Thy Will, O God

*L*ord, let Your will be my surrender;
Make this stubborn heart by grace more tender.
May I draw from Thee, O Sovereign Lender,
All power over sin that is Thine to render.
Let Thy mercies past be mine to remember;
Grant strength and solace, my sure Defender.
Keep the warmth of Your love a burning ember.
Thy will be done. Let nothing hinder!

Heart Prayer

*L*ord,
Move on my heart.
Place within my heart,
Hammer upon my heart,
Pierce my heart
With the desire
To do your will.
Not only
To do it,
But to do it
Willingly.

"... Your will be done
On earth as it is in heaven."
Matthew 6:10

Prayer: Use Us, Lord

*L*ord, keep us willing
To be used of You,
To serve and bless
Another.
Keep us pressing on
And breaking through
The cocoon of self
That smothers.
The cocoon that wraps
Us warm and tight
So comfortable
At times.
But so imprisons,
So impairs the sight
That we see
Only me.
Me, myself and mine.
Lord, keep us free
From the futility
Of that inward,
Empty place.
Release from self,
From apathy.
Use us by
Your grace.

"... with goodwill doing service, as to the Lord,
and not to men." Ephesians 6:7

Hope in God
(Hope for Parents)

Hope in God; exult in His glory above.
As did the faithful witnesses of all the ages past.
In hope against hope, await for Him to move
And draw the far-sailed prodigal to salvation shores at last.

Hope in God; there is no other hope.
In confident expectation await His mighty hand
To reach, to grasp, to send love's gospel rope
To rescue and deliver the wave-tossed one to land.

Hope in God; He desires that none should drown
In blackened seas of sin, in world-capped waters deep.
For our floundering sons and daughters, His Son wore Calvary's crown
And He resurrected lives --- to save and sanctify and keep!

Felled

*T*all, strong, immoveable, for decades it stood,
With high arching branches of gnarled wood.
But then came a sudden summer storm,
And the tree lay uprooted, lifeless, forlorn.
It had offered shelter and welcoming shade
To all who under it had sat and played.
Thus, as it lay felled across the grass,
It brought sighs and tears to many who passed.
Strange. The loss of a tree to be such sorrow source.
Yet, men's lives are felled daily without any remorse.
And infant lives uprooted. Lives of great potential.
An act of violence, yet to many inconsequential.

*"And God said to Noah, 'The end of all flesh has
come before Me, for the earth is filled with
violence through them; and behold,
I will destroy them with the earth.'"
Genesis 6:13*

Much

To whom much is given
Much is required.
But what does much mean
From our point of view?

Sad how little is much
From our perspective,
And how little the much
That we do.

"For everyone to whom much is given,
from him much will be required."
Luke 12:48

The Sword of the Spirit

We know
Without a doubt
That Satan roams about
Seeking whom
He may devour.
We also know
To be true
That we, too,
Have power,
Through the Word,
To deplete
His power,
And the enemy
Defeat.
Please,
Please, dear Lord,
Keep reminding
Us to wield
Your sword.
We so often
Forget
Only to be
Caught in
Satan's net.

Ephesians 6:1-17

War in These Last Days

I remember war.
War back when
War's one purpose
Was to defend
Our nation.
War was
Different then.
We knew the enemy.
We killed only our foes.
Now, evil men hate
And even kill those
With whom they merely disagree.
There is no hope.
For America
It's so plain to see,
Until we,
As a nation,
Repent.
Repent and
Bow the knee.

"But evil men and impostors will grow worse
and worse, deceiving and being deceived."
2 Timothy 3:13

"... The kingdom of God is at hand.
Repent, and believe in the gospel."
Mark 1:15

Unprofitable Servants

*L*ord,
Unprofitable servants, we.
Help us in our pride to see
That we cannot begin
To boast.
Even when and where
We have succeeded most.
We, of ourselves,
Can nothing be
Or do.
We are wholly dependent
On grace from You.
As dutiful servants,
Let honor be our goal.
Honor only
To the One
Who saved our soul.

*So likewise you, when you have done all
those things which you are commanded,
say, "We are unprofitable servants.
We have done what was our duty to do."
Luke 17:10*

Unbusy

*L*ord, I know that You
Are pleased
When I do
The work that You
Have called me to.
I know that in
Your Word You say,
"Work while it is day,"
For the dark of night
Is not far away.
But Lord, I think
You must, at times,
Be pleased, too,
When for an hour,
Or perhaps a few,
On a bright
And glorious day,
I sit on my porch
In my rocking chair
And nothing do.
Nothing --- but
Sit and stare.
And revel in
Your creation.
My heart filled
With appreciation.

"Oh, that men would give thanks
to the LORD for His goodness,
and for His wonderful works
to the children of men!"
Psalm 107:31

Prayer For Perseverance

*W*hen troubles mount to trials, may my worship never cease.
When those I hold most precious shun Your presence and Your peace.
When afflictions flog with weighted thong,
May my trembling lips lift praise and song.
Oh, Savior of my soul most dear,
I seek through You to persevere.

I seek to persevere, Lord, through a grasp upon Your grace,
And through Your Word and power run the challenge of Your race.
Thus, experience by my trial attained,
The character of Your Son is gained.
Then hope, that virtue, oh, so dear
Appears --- when I have persevered.

And hope will disappoint not, for it cannot ever fail.
Merged in love it's measured; by the love of God availed.
As by faith it came, in faith results,
By grace I stand, in hope exult.
In hope, in love, Oh, Savior dear,
I seek through You to persevere.

With hope I share Your gospel and with hope I deem it heard,
For the power that lies within it is the power of Your Word.
As with hope I pray and intercede
That You set the captive free indeed,
Dear Lord, as fast Your Day draws near,
I need Your strength to persevere.

Romans 5:3-5

Your Names in My Trials

*A*h, sovereign God, You're the Lord of my trials.
You're the Lord of Lords. Exalted is Your Name.
You are Faithful and True. Your delays are not denials.
Your names endure forever. No others are the same.

Your name is El Roi, "The God Who Sees."
You watch over and keep me in every sudden plight.
You're El Roi o'er my fears, and from my fears You free.
There is hope in Your presence, courage from Your sight.

Your name is Jehovah-shammah, "The God Who Is There."
You are there, ever there, in all my desperate need.
You're Jehovah-raah, "Lord My Shepherd" Who cares.
My Shepherd there to guide, my Shepherd there to lead.

Your name is El Elyon, You're "The God Most High."
You rule over all the universe, all the realms of mortal men.
Your love and rule sustain me 'til death draws my final sigh,
And throughout my earthly sojourn, You restore me once again.

Your name is Jehovah-jireh, "The Lord Will Provide."
Your bountiful provision flows freely from Your throne.
New mercies, new strength, when sorrows flood like the tide.
Your compassions they fail not because I'm Your own.

Your name is Jehovah-shalom, "The Lord Is Peace."
So precious that name in the solemn depth of night.
Peace from Your Word. By Your Spirit sweet release,
Passing all understanding, my grateful soul's delight.

The name of Jesus! Name above all names!
Wonderful Counselor, Almighty God Who saves.
There's power in Your name; eternal it will reign.
And I'll share my Savior's victory o'er sin and o'er the grave.

Ah sovereign God, You name's a strong tower.
The righteous run to it in all their distress.
To Your name belong praise, honor, glory, and power.
It matters not the trial, in Your name I am blessed.

"The name of the LORD is a strong tower;
The righteous run to it and are safe."
Proverbs 18:10

Unforgiveness

*W*hy do people bitter-barbed and ugly fences build?
And horrid, hateful, high, thick walls?
Care they so little about God's holy will
And His unceasing call
Not to just a few, but to all,
To follow in the steps of Jesus the loving, forgiving Lord?
Love they, cherish they, very most of all
What God forbids? Oh, sad, sad rebellion ---
Never by Him unnoticed, never ever small!
'Tis rebellion once --- in Eden ---
Caused the fall.

*"But if you do not forgive,
neither will your Father in heaven
forgive your trespasses."
Mark 11:26*

Perspective

I perceive the reality
Of this life's brevity
From a perspective unique
To advancing age.
Childhood. Youth. The middle years.
All coming full circle
At sunset stage.

It's as one who views
The earth from space.
Seeing from afar
The whole grand sphere.
It's seeing through the lens
Of a life long lived
Birth. Death. Between,
Some allotted years.

It's gratitude for grace
Growing ever deeper.
It's amazement at God's mercy
As life is reviewed.
It's gaining compassion,
More caring for others.
Praying for mind and strength
To be renewed.

→

It's perceiving God's sovereignty
Over all things.
While fast is approaching
My "dust to dust."
It's praising God more
For so great a salvation,
And trusting yet more
The Lord
That I trust.

"Even to your old age, I am He,
And even to gray hairs
I will carry you! ..."
Isaiah 46:4

Oh To Be a Tree

Oh to be a tree planted by rivers of water.
Oh to have roots buried deep in the ground.
Oh to stand tall when surrounded by sinners.
Oh to know truth, to hold doctrine that's sound.

Never to walk in the counsel of the ungodly.
Never to sit in the seat of the one who scorns.
Always to bring forth fruit in its season.
To meditate on the Word as each day is born.

To delight in the Lord when day is closing.
To be thankful and worship Him faithfully ever.
To be a tree sturdy that will shelter others.
Whose leaf remains green and shall not wither.

"Blessed is the man
Who walks not in the counsel of the ungodly,
Nor stands in the path of sinners,
Nor sits in the seat of the scornful;
But his delight is in the law of the LORD,
And in His law he meditates day and night.
He shall be like a tree
Planted by the rivers of water,
That brings forth its fruit in its season,
Whose leaf also shall not wither;
And whatever he does shall prosper."
Psalm 1:1-3

God's Transforming Power

*B*efore the sun arises in a burst of golden red,
"Three times you will deny Me," the loving Master said.
He knew the inner longing of the one so quick to say
That his life he would lay down for Jesus every day.

But when the sun soon ascended in glorious fashion,
When the cock loudly crowed with heralding passion,
Peter stood no longer at the Master's side.
Instead, in fear and faithlessness his Savior he denied.

Yet on down the years this great apostle brave,
In humble service to his Lord his life he freely gave.
When God had finally finished with this rough-hewn man,
Peter's promise was fulfilled by God's prophetic plan.

Amazing how the Lord can take and shape and mold
And utterly transform a man. Amazing to behold!
Oh, the delightful expectation, the hope of each one newly-born,
Though our yearnings be not yet yieldings, God will mightily transform.

All Kinds of Blessings

*B*lessings as many as the sands of the sea.
Blessings as numerous as the stars in the sky.
What sunlit seashore, what broad constellation
Can contain the whole of God's vast supply?

Blessings from the past not now remembered.
Blessings in the future. Myriads to come.
Blessings in eternity every passing moment.
Many today before setting sun.

Blessings received with praise and thanksgiving.
Yet so many unseen, so many ignored.
All undeserved from our gracious Savior.
All because of the love of our gracious Lord.

Blessings of trials, blessings of sorrows.
Blessings unwanted; they come in disguise.
But later in time, revealed and discovered
To be His very best from our God all-wise.

"Happy are the people
whose God is the LORD!"
Psalm 144:15

Goodness and Mercy

Surely goodness and mercy
Shall follow me
All the days of
My pilgrimage here.
Surely goodness and mercy
Shall follow me
Through the darkest of days
When my trials are severe.

Surely goodness and mercy
Shall follow me
When ominous clouds
On the horizon appear.
Surely goodness and mercy
Shall never less be
When the challenge is great
And many the fears.

Surely goodness and mercy
Shall follow me
When I search for clear paths
Yet my path lies unclear.
Surely goodness and mercy
Will available be
When I know the Lord is speaking
But I struggle to hear.

Surely goodness and mercy
Shall follow me.
The mere sound of the words
Is precious and dear.
Surely goodness and mercy
I will know, I will see
In more fullness
As closer
I to Jesus draw near.

"Surely goodness and mercy
shall follow me
All the days of my life..."
Psalm 23:6

So Great a Salvation

So Great a Salvation

*L*ord, in all the beauty
Of Your creation
Your magnificence is
Not hard to see.
But greater far the beauty
Of Your redemption
When Christ came to dwell
In sinful me.

Lord, I see the power
Of Your creation
From majestic peak
To foaming sea.
Greater still the power
Of Your salvation
When You transform
A sinner.
A sinner like me.

*"How shall we escape if we neglect
so great a salvation..."*
Hebrews 2:3

Chasing the Wind

Chasing the wind.
Such a frivolous pursuit
That neither common sense
Nor logic can defend.
Yet, neglecting our souls,
We choose that fatal route.
And there is no happy,
No hopeful end
When we choose
To chase the wind.
Chasing the wind
Is living life in vain.
There's no eternal profit
To study, work or play.
No assurance to the soul
Can anything temporal lend,
As we exist in a world
Of sin
And fear
And pain.
We've no gracious,
Sovereign Lord to trust
As our aging bodies
Return to dust.
Ultimately they fail
To mend,
And we keep chasing
After the wind.

Chasing the wind
Is running to seize
Hurricane's gust
Or some elusive breeze
To keep, to clasp.
It's finding no absolutes
To grasp.
Oh, the danger
When pride
And deception blend.
As we continue in
Our folly
Of chasing,
Ever chasing
After the wind.

"Chasing the Wind"
Ecclesiastes 6:9 (KJV)

"Do not be wise in your own eyes;
Fear the LORD and depart from evil."
Proverbs 3:7

Something More
(Salvation)

An inner searching,
An inner yearning,
An inner deep desire,
For something more,
For something true,
For something so much higher.

An inner emptiness,
An inner restlessness,
An inner, quiet despair,
A need for something,
A need for Someone
Who always will be there.

An inner peace now,
An inner hope now,
An inner change for all
Who find new life,
Who find new rest,
Who answer Jesus' call.

*"Come to Me, all you who labor and are
heavy laden, and I will give you rest."*
Matthew 11:28

Eternity

*I*n eternity present, man makes a choice
To heed or ignore the Lord's Sovereign voice.
Each is accountable <u>now</u> to decide
Whether in heaven or hell he will reside.

In eternity present, fearful, insecure
Nations strive to conquer, to even endure.
Wars increase and rumors of war.
Men trust in their weapons instead of the Lord.

In eternity present, the present grows late.
Men's hearts abound with anger and hate.
On this troubled globe, no peace but One.
The Prince of Peace, God's beloved Son.

In eternity present, God has given His grace,
And time to repent for the whole human race.
God gives witness of Jesus and infallible proofs.
God gives us the Scriptures to reveal His Truth.

In eternity future, He'll return to earth
No longer as servant of humble birth.
He'll come as Judge, not advocate.
But sadly, for many it will be too late.

In eternity now, we pray and we plead
For God to open the eyes of all who read.
<u>Now</u>, while you're blessed with life and breath,
Trust Jesus for victory over sin, over death!

"He who believes in the Son has everlasting life;
and he who does not believe the Son shall not see life,
but the wrath of God abides on him." John 3:36

By Grace You Are Saved Through Faith

*N*o man is justified
By the works of the Law
In God's sight.
Yet, in our sad plight
We strive to keep the Law.
To do another good deed
We think will plead
Our case with God.
But instead,
By the Law
We are led
To reject His grace.
We think we can,
As sinful man,
Somehow find space
In heaven's broad place
By our own good works,
By our own plan.
How pathetic
This plan
We have selected.
While God's own plan,
And Jesus,
And grace
We have rejected.

"... knowing that a man is not justified by the works of the law but by faith in Jesus Christ..."   Galatians 2:16

"For by grace you have been saved through faith, and that not of yourselves; it is the gift of God, not of works, lest anyone should boast. For we are His workmanship, created in Christ Jesus for good works, which God prepared beforehand that we should walk in them." Ephesians 2:8-10

No Mere Words

*C*an anyone articulate
The miracle of salvation?
Can human words describe
This wholly divine
Event in time?
Its resurrection powers?
Has ever been vocabulary
Could illustrate
How in a moment
Of a day, of an hour,
A soul is rescued
From its dreadful,
Dark and sinful state?
What dictionary
Over the ages
Has contained words
To define,
Among its pages,
What is not a matter
Of intellect or mind
But wholly of spirit?
The miracle by which
The soul inherits
New life, and the old
Is left behind.

→

No. No mere words
Can possibly convey
The glories of salvation.
No. Not even from the one
Who receives it
And is blessed
By its transformation.

"But we all, with unveiled face,
beholding as in a mirror
the glory of the Lord,
are being transformed
into the same image
from glory to glory,
just as by the
Spirit of the Lord."
2 Corinthians 3:18

Unfallen

*A*s raindrops fall from heaven
To mingle with spring's soft breeze,
As leaves fall down in autumn
From multicolored trees,
As petals fall in summer
From the flowers they adorn,
As snowflakes fall to frozen earth
During winter's blustery storm,
Mankind, too, is fallen, fallen
And needs to be reborn.
Ever since the fall in Eden,
Man's fall has been ever down.
Born to live a little while,
Then destined to a grave in the ground.
But Lord, Your call to fallen man
Is so loving and gracious and so grand.
Your call is to upward, upward soar,
Up to heaven's lovely land.
Up to rise and fall no more.
This Lord, Your greatest blessing,
Your marvelous, merciful call.
You and You alone, Lord.
You reversed the Fall!

Genesis Chapter 3

*"... Proclaim the praises of Him
Who called you out of darkness
into His marvelous light."
1 Peter 2:9*

Time and Tide

*S*omeone once said
That time and tide
Wait for no man.
This none has denied
Nor ever can.
Try halting the waves
Or stopping the sun.
Yet God these very things
Has done.
Time and tide
Against all men flow,
But if the sovereign God
They serve and know,
Those who walk
With the Lord
And are on His side,
Need not fear
Either
Time nor tide.

"So the sun stood still, And the moon stopped..."
Joshua 10:13

"Then He (Jesus) arose and rebuked the wind,
and said to the sea, 'Peace, be still!'"
Mark 4:39

Life is a Vapor

*P*uffs of steam
From a teakettle pour.
A fine mist drenches
Morning with dew.
Fog obscures a landscape.
All appear for a time
Then disappear quickly
From our view.
Life is a vapor.
This the Scriptures
Teach, with warnings say.
It appears for a time,
Then it vanishes away.
No one knows
What time or day.
God has put eternity
In the hearts of men.
But men ignore it.
And then,
When
Eternity appears
It appears to stay.

"... you do not know what will happen tomorrow.
For what is your life? It is even a vapor that appears
for a little time and then vanishes away." James 4:14

"... He has put eternity in their hearts..." Ecclesiastes 3:11

Joy of a Soul Won

*T*he many hours
That we pray,
The encouraging words
That we say,
The Christ-like deeds
That we may do
To meet another's needs.
These provide joy.
But sometimes
Disappointment too.
Sometimes serving the Lord
Is quite hard.
There is so much self
To disregard.
But there is one thing
We do under the sun
That brings lasting joy.
It's the soul that we've won.
It also brings rejoicing
Before the throne of our Father.
It is a joy unspeakable.
It is like no other.

"Serve the LORD with gladness..." Psalm 100:2

*"Likewise, I say to you, there is joy in the presence
of the angels of God over one sinner who repents."
Luke 15:10*

Just One Moment

I heard one night that a Redeemer lives.
I heard He's God's Son and He'll eternally reign.
I heard that He died to save me, a sinner,
I heard I could trust no other name.
I believed by the hearing of my ear.
I believed by the seeing of my eyes.
I understood in my heart He offered salvation.
That for me Christ was born, that for me He died.
I believed at just one moment the message I heard.
I believed just one moment one miraculous night.
Then into my life came my Savior and Lord.
Into my life came the Truth, the Life, the Light.
Into my life at one moment He came to reign.
In just that one moment I was born again.
One moment lost, a sinner bound for hell.
The next moment God's child, with Him forever to dwell.
Though it has been many years, I remember it well.
I cannot keep silent. The good news I still tell.

*"... if you confess with your mouth the Lord Jesus
and believe in your heart that God has raised Him
from the dead, you will be saved. For with the
heart one believes unto righteousness, and with
the mouth confession is made unto salvation."*
Romans 10:9-10

*"Jesus said ..., 'I am the way, the truth, and the life.
No one comes to the Father except through Me.'"*
John 14:6

Praise for the Blessed Narrow Gate

I was a sheep in arid pastures wandering.
I had no shepherd to guide me. My sin was very great.
Then the Good Shepherd Who gave His life for me
Found me and led me through the blessed narrow gate.

I was a sheep in fear and doubt and confusion,
I was most unaware of my sinful, lost state.
I kept grazing in thorn-infested meadows,
Followed a road that led straight through the very wide gate.

I was lost but at times for truth was searching.
As a young lamb had seen much anger, much hate.
I sought answers to questions no one could answer
Until I followed the Shepherd through the blessed narrow gate.

I was a sheep growing hopeless; my life seemed empty.
Long years did the Shepherd watch over me, wait.
Then one life-changing evening He called me to Him.
He called me and led me through the blessed narrow gate.

Now I'm a sheep guided by the Good Shepherd,
The Good Shepherd Whose love will never abate.
He will feed me forever in the greenest of pastures.
Praise the One Who leads through the blessed narrow gate!

Jesus said, "I am the Good Shepherd.
The Good Shepherd gives His life for the sheep."
John 10:11

"Enter by the narrow gate; for wide is the gate
and broad is the way that leads to destruction."
Matthew 7:13

One Eventful Day

*I*t was in the city of Philippi
On one eventful day,
That Paul went down to the riverside
And on its shady banks espied
Some women meeting to pray.
Paul readily preached the gospel,
And her Savior Lydia received.
What joy for the dear apostle
When all her household believed!
A church was quickly planted.
And though at first quite small,
It had the Lord's most godly shepherd,
None other than His servant Paul.
But in the city of Philippi
The gospel must not stay.
Paul spread it to other cities
On other eventful days.
Many centuries later,
It came to America's shores,
And after many years had passed,
I, too, received the Lord.
Like Lydia before me,
I believed. I prayed. And then
On one special, eventful day
I was born again.

→

I like to think quite often
Of my historic riverside
When Jesus entered into my life
Eternally to abide.
It was my most eventful day,
It was my most eventful place,
When I saw that Jesus is the Way,
And He saved me by His grace.

Acts Chapter 16

Infinity

*N*o human reasoning
Can reach it
Or clasp it.
No stretch of the intellect
Will ever grasp it.
Thus, many view it
With apprehension,
This matter beyond
Mortal comprehension.
Yet, all in infinity
Will ultimately dwell.
This the Scriptures
Plainly tell.
But where, where
In infinity?
We have but two choices:
Heaven or hell.
In one or the other
We'll forever remain.
This the Scriptures
Make ever so plain.
It matters not
What we think or feel.
It matters only
What the Scriptures reveal.
If we believe the gospel
That the Scriptures relate,
Then infinity is pure joy
To contemplate.

"... Christ died for our sins according to the Scriptures, and ... He was buried, and ... He rose again the third day according to the Scriptures..."   1 Corinthians 15:3-4

Someday! One Day!

*S*omeday, one day, should I arise
To raptured glory through trumpeted skies,
Not a backward glance, not a tear nor lament
That this earthly pilgrimage fully is spent.

Someday, one day, instead, should I die
To be present with Jesus, to His arms I will fly.
He saved me from darkness to walk in His light,
To abide with Him ever --- Oh, glorious flight!

One day by Rapture, or one day by death,
This mortal being will breathe my last breath.
And put on immortal and ascend to God's throne,
Ne'er to weep nor to sorrow in the perfection of home.

One day through the heavens my spirit shall soar
With joy inexpressible at beholding my Lord.
Oh, the thought of that meeting --- of seeing His face!
Oh, the thought of the love of His eternal embrace!

Someday! One day! For that day I prepare
By serving my Savior, by study, by prayer.
By new mercies each morning, by His infinite grace,
By His plan divine, in His perfect time, I will finish the race.

"I have fought the good fight,
I have finished the race,
I have kept the faith."
2 Timothy 4:7

His Servant Simeon

*T*here was a man in centuries gone
Who was old and dim of sight.
The name of the man was Simeon,
And his beard was long and white.

Devout he was, though nearing death,
But as few in all his nation,
He yearned to see while he yet had breath,
Israel's consolation.

The Holy Spirit him a message gave
As he waited patiently,
That this humble servant before the grave
Messiah truly would see.

Though frail of flesh, his faith was strong.
Oh, a peculiar man was he.
To the religious crowd he did not belong.
In his heart was eternity.

It came to pass in God's own time,
That on one glorious morn
That Simeon beheld a sight sublime,
The infant newly born.

The age-gnarled hands held tight the child
In grateful adoration.
With tears of joy he wept --- he smiled,
"Mine eyes have seen my salvation!"

→

"Sovereign Lord, I have seen Your Light!
Let Your servant depart in peace.
The glory of Israel in all people's sight,
I've beheld Him face to face!"

Are **you** awaiting as Simeon, my friend,
The Lord your eyes to behold?
Are you prepared as the age nears its end
To greet Him with confidence bold?

Does your spirit desire, do you fervently pray
For the Master's soon return?
Are your affections set on that glorious day
As for His appearance you yearn?

Or, have you not heard the Sovereign call,
That before this earth you leave
You must give to Jesus your life, your all,
You must repent of sin and believe?

Lord, grant us hearts so faithful, so pure
That we long for our Savior's face.
Lord, keep us singleminded and sure.
Make us Simeons strong by your grace!

Luke 2:25-32

Christmas

Jesus, The Light Of Christmas

<u>Darkness --- Separation from God</u>

Sin, rebellion towards God

Envy

Pride

Allegiance to other gods

Religion without Lordship

Anger, unforgiveness

Trusting in one's own goodness

Immoral thoughts, words, deeds

Opposition to God's Word

No repentance for sin

<u>Jesus --- Life</u>

Joy of salvation in Him

Eternal life through Him

Sins forgiven by Him

Union with God because of Him

Salvation's blessings from Him

→

Jesus --- Light

Righteousness from God
Everlasting life with God
Christ as Wonderful Counselor
Overcoming sin and death
Never forsaken, never alone
Christ as Intercessor
Indwelling Holy Spirit
Love of God
Inward transformation
A brand new birth
Truth for life
Immanuel --- God with us
Out of darkness
No condemnation

*Jesus said, "I am the Way, the Truth, and the Life.
No one comes to the Father but by me."
John 14:6*

*Jesus said, "I am the light of the world.
He who follows Me shall not walk in
darkness but have the light of life."
John 8:12*

Immanuel (God with us) Came

Immanuel came! What a joy to proclaim
The good tidings of God's gift of glory!
The wee babe in the straw replaced grace for the Law.
History surrenders to the power of His story.

Immanuel came --- to the praise of His name!
Came to offer us peace deep within.
The dear child in the stall came to die for us all ---
All are sinners dark-stained with our sin.

Immanuel came! On the cross bled for our shame.
He was buried and raised to God's throne.
The child born that night, Lord triumphant in might,
In love beckons to bring sinners home.

Immanuel came! And we're never the same
Who in repentance the Scriptures believe,
Trust the One from the stable as the **only** One able
To save us --- and death's fears relieve.

Immanuel came! He's hope's bright burning flame.
In a world mired in darkness and strife.
Immanuel's King! Oh, His high praises sing!
Bow! Receive Him! And give Him your life!

"Therefore the Lord himself shall give you a sign;
Behold, a virgin shall conceive, and bear a son,
and shall call his name Immanuel."
Isaiah 7:14

Jesus, The Eternal God

*I*n eternity past, Jesus was there.
With God He created everywhere.
He **was** God, Creator of everything.
He **is** God. God the Savior, God the King.

In centuries past, to a far-off land.
Jesus left heaven to become Son of Man.
The Son of God came to earth to dwell
As God with man, Immanuel.

In centuries past, Mary's infant child
Came to serve a world by sin defiled.
He grew to manhood, God's perfect Man.
He died for sinners, God's perfect plan.

In centuries past, the grave could not hold
The triumphant Jesus, as prophets foretold.
He arose! He lives! He reigns! He rules!
To resist His call is to play the fool.

In eternity present, Jesus sits on His throne.
He calls a world of sinners to become His own.
All have sinned in rebellion and pride.
For the love of them all, He was crucified.

In eternity present, there is but a while
For man with God to be reconciled.
Christ, the Way to God, one Way alone
Is calling, "Come now! Come sinner, come home!"

In eternity present, man makes a choice
To heed or ignore the Lord's sovereign voice.
Each is accountable now to decide
Whether in heaven or hell he'll forever reside.

In eternity present, fearful…insecure
Nations strive to conquer, to even endure.
Wars increase and rumors of war.
Men trust in their weapons instead of the Lord.

In eternity present, the present grows late.
Men's hearts abound with anger and hate.
On this troubled globe, no peace but One.
The Prince of Peace, God's beloved Son.

In eternity present, God has given His grace,
And time to repent for the whole human race.
God gives witness of Jesus and infallible proofs.
God gives us the Scriptures to reveal His Truth.

In eternity future, He'll return to earth
No longer as servant of humble birth.
He'll come as Judge, not advocate.
But sadly, for many it will be too late.

In eternity now, we pray and we plead
For God to open the eyes of all who read.
Now, while you're blessed with life and breath,
Trust Jesus for victory over sin, over death!

*"In the beginning was the Word, and the Word was with God,
and the Word was God. All things came into being by Him,
and apart from Him nothing came into being that has come
into being." John 1:1-2*

"Death is swallowed up in victory." 1 Corinthians 15:54

The Question for All Seasons

*T*here is a question that hovers ever
Over the freshly fallen snow;
That permeates the frigid air
Invades the season with lights aglow:
When this and all seasons of life are over,
Where, oh where, dear soul, will you go?

God Himself asks the ultimate question.
God Himself requires your reply.
Are you preparing for eternity
As your years go hastening by?
Do you know why Jesus came down to earth?
That for you He came to die?

God Himself asks the critical question.
As Creator it is His to ask.
He is the King of Kings, He's Lord of Lords.
Only His sovereign rule will last.
Ponder long and carefully the answer, dear one.
Before your opportunity is passed.

God's Son shed His blood on Calvary's cross.
God, out of love, sent Him there to die.
Out of love Jesus gave His life for sinners.
Then God raised from the dead the Crucified.
He paid your sin's penalty. He paid the full cost.
Now sits the Savior at His Father's side.

God Himself asks the crucial question
Of all He's given breath to breathe.
He holds all accountable as to their reply.
Have they His beloved Son received?
Heaven is for those who follow Jesus.
Hell is for the ones by Satan deceived.

What will you give for your soul, dear one?
What can you give in exchange for your soul?
God declares that the wages of sin is death.
Eternal and tragic is sin's terrible toll.
But payment was offered by the blood of God's Son.
Jesus is Redeemer. Jesus makes whole.

God's question at Christmas as darkness surrounds us,
As life's relentless winds blow fierce and wild,
Will you surrender your life to the loving Savior?
Will you repent, believe, become God's child?
Come. Receive forgiveness and new life in Jesus.
The hour grows short. Come! Be reconciled.

Jesus said, "I am the Way, the Truth, and the Life.
No one comes to the Father except through Me."
John 14:6

Seek the Lord While He May Be Found

*T*he old year is waning, and a new year is dawning.
Houses lie huddled under icicle awnings.
Flurries fog the Christmas lights and muffle Christmas sounds.
And ever clear is the reminder: "Seek the Lord while He may be found."

Seek the Lord Jesus. Seek the Lord of humble birth.
The Babe laid in a manger is Lord of heaven and earth.
Lowly shepherds that first Christmas went seeking Him and found
God's promised gift of the Savior in a small Judean town.

Wise men also came seeking; from the East they traveled far.
They had riches and much learning and faithfully followed a star
Until they found the Christ child, Lord and King over all the nations.
They adored and worshiped their Messiah there, and there received salvation.

Seek the Lord, seek the Lord, whether of low or high estate.
Seek Him now. Seek His salvation before it is too late.
If you seek Him, you will find Him, if you seek with all your heart.
There's none other Who can save you, nor such great love impart.

A tragic destiny awaits those who seek other in His place;
Their lives spent in futility without His mercy and His grace.
To seek earth's temporal offerings is but a chasing of the wind.
There's no real peace, there's no real hope, no deliverance from sin.

Some go seeking after riches; and their gain comes with great cost.
There's dissatisfaction in their increase, devastation at their loss.
Some go seeking after fame, but fame is fleeting in its flight,
And it breeds a secret loneliness piercing even at its height.

Some seek worldly pleasures, but all pleasures do grow dim,
And the ceaseless grasping for them sows much discontent within.
Some seek the world's religions. Each has idols all its own.
Each offers a grand deception until death and hell are won.

So many souls are seeking; they know not what nor where.
All around is mass confusion, anxiety and fear.
The news grows more alarming filled with violence, wars and grief,
And the solutions of mere mortals cannot provide relief.

"Seek the Lord," the Scriptures tell us. "Seek Him while He is near."
Seek Him in times of trouble --- in loss, in sorrow, fear.
Seek and you will find Him --- this, the good news of God's Word.
Seek the only eternal Truth the weary world has ever heard.

Seek Him and receive Him. Seek Him to become His own.
He will cleanse you. He will guide you. You will never be alone.
Seek the infinite, almighty Savior, for He is God come down
To save you, heal you, bring you peace. Seek Him while He may be found.

It's Christmas and the old, old message rings over the wintry ground.
It's Christmas and this message will ever be the sweetest sound.
Jesus died for sinners, lost, lonely, despairing, bound.
Seek Jesus, only Jesus. Seek Him while He may be found.

"Seek the Lord while He may be found..."
Isaiah 55:6

"And you will seek Me and find Me,
when you search for Me
with all your heart."
Jeremiah 29:13

Jesus, God's Gift of Mercy

Mercy triumphed over justice
One star-strewn night in Bethlehem
When God, in mercy, sent His Son as Savior
To this world of undeserving men.

Mercy triumphed over justice
When all that the prophets long foretold
Was fulfilled that night in an ancient city.
God came in the flesh for flesh to behold.

Mercy triumphed over justice.
God's love, grace and mercy were all combined
In the gift of the long-awaited Messiah,
The light and hope of all mankind.

Mercy triumphed over justice
Where a cross later stood on Jerusalem's hill,
When Jesus the Savior bled and died there
In obedience to His Father's will.

Mercy triumphed over justice
When Jesus, victorious, arose from the grave.
Sin, Satan, death --- all were defeated,
And all who would receive Him as Lord were saved.

Mercy yet triumphs over justice.
Jesus yet calls. Each one has a choice
As He sets before us blessing and cursing,
Life and death. Hear now His voice!

Mercy yet triumphs over justice.
Why do many choose justice when mercy avails?
God is holy and just. Their sin will condemn them.
But for those who repent, God's mercy prevails.

Mercy triumphs over justice.
Christmas ever reminds of the eternal good news.
The Scriptures proclaim God's merciful offer:
Justice or Jesus? Which one will you choose?

"... I have set before you life and death,
blessing and cursing;
therefore choose life, ..."
Deuteronomy 30:19

Jesus Is the Door

*I*t's a season of snow and homes aglow with Christmas decorations.
A season when bargains beckon and busy shoppers crowd the stores.
When God trumpets to the nations the soul's need for salvation.
"The soul that sinneth, it shall die." But Jesus is the door.

It's a season of memories that span the many years.
They're a tapestry tight-woven of youth and childhood lore.
For some, fond recollection; for others, remembrances with tears.
But what must never be forgotten is that Jesus is the door.

It's a time of reflection upon a year that's fading fast.
Long thoughts flood the mind as waves flood the shore.
Fleeting time, the great reminder this temporal will not last.
Now the time to embrace the eternal truth: That Jesus is the door.

It's the season to contemplate the dear Savior's birth.
The One Who on a cross of death the sins of mankind bore.
To a world of dying sinners God sent His Son to die on earth.
Then raised Him triumphant from the grave. Victor! Savior! Door!

This door through all centuries is in Scripture described.
The door to life eternal — as never since or ever before!
On that first Christmas night when the infant first cried,
God gave the world its greatest gift. He gave Jesus as the door.

Because Jesus is God Who came in the form of a man,
There is no greater love on lost sinners outpoured.
There is no greater miracle, this gracious perfect plan,
God's opening of heaven's portal. Jesus is the door.

There is an entrance to glory for the one who will repent.
Who will turn from sin to live for Him, the sovereign Lord of Lords.
Who will humbly serve the Son God so mercifully has sent.
Who will come to God the only way. Jesus only is the door.

It's the season for the good news to be gratefully received.
God's eternal wrath is certain should salvation be ignored.
It's the season of rejoicing for those who trust Him and believe.
Who worship the Christ, Messiah and King. Who enter through the door.

It's the season of the message that through the ages has endured.
A tumultuous future approaches; no one can know what lies in store.
But the Word of the Lord is eternal, and its hope remains secure.
The trumpet call resounds loudly to all. Jesus is the door!

Jesus said. "I am the door.
If anyone enters by Me,
he will be saved."
John 10:9

Jesus, The Light of the World

The people that walked in darkness have seen a great light.
A light no celestial stars provide,
Nor moon in fullness circling wide.
Nor radiant, burning, beaming sun.
The light is the light of a man, the One
Whom God in mercy and grace bestowed
Upon this sin-dark world below.
A light to light the lives of men,
To reconcile them back to Him.
If they would but receive this One
Whose name is Jesus, God's own Son.

For the people who walk in darkness and see **not** the great light,
Persistent God's call, though never redundant:
Come!   Come to Jesus for life abundant.
He's the light that pierces sin's domain.
Sole balm for soul's suffering, sadness, pain.
For the fear-bound He's offer of trust and peace,
For the doubt-imprisoned, faith's sweet release.
He's the light that dispels the dread of death.
He's eternal life at life's last breath.
He's the hope of Christmas down the centuries told,
God's gift of the Savior and the light of the world.

*"But as many as received Him, to them He gave
the right to become children of God, to those
who believe in His name." John 1:12*

*"The people that walked in darkness
have seen a great light..." Isaiah 9:2*

118

Jesus, The King of Kings

*A*ll heaven and earth are Jesus' dominion.
And all the vast universe around and between.
God sent His Son to a Bethlehem stable.
His Son would be Prophet and Priest and King.

God sent Jesus as servant and Savior.
He grew Him in stature, the young Nazarene.
He led Him to Calvary to die there for sinners.
Then He raised Him to reign as victorious King.

Jesus reigns over earthly terror and conflict.
In tumult and tempest we can praise Him and sing.
His peace will sustain all who obey and adore Him.
He's the Prince of Peace. He's the sovereign King.

All heaven and earth are the King's dominion.
And life. And death. These are no small thing.
The choice is ours---His mercy or judgment.
There's no greater tragedy than to reject the King.

Yes, Jesus reigns in eternal dominion.
To weary sinners a solace He brings.
To those who repent He offers forgiveness.
To those who will follow and honor the King.

Jesus will return. There's a Second Coming.
For those who love Him, how glorious a thing.
He desires every heart to bow to His Lordship.
Now is the accepted time. Receive now the King.

"He is Lord of lords and King of kings." Rev 17:14

"Behold, now is the accepted time; behold, now is the day of salvation." 2 Corinthians 6:2

Who Is the Jesus of Christmas?

*T*here are bright colored lights in the city.
There are bright colored lights in the town.
There is music and hurried activity.
There is snow wafting down to the ground.
But where is the Jesus of Christmas,
Son of God of so little renown?

There is much festivity in the city.
There is much festivity in the town.
The decorations are oh, so pretty!
And Christmas is everywhere found.
But where is the Jesus of Christmas,
Son of God of so little renown?

Families gather in homes in the city.
Families gather in homes in the town.
But are they gathering in love and in His peace
Or do strife and discord abound?
Where is Jesus in the family at Christmas,
Son of God of so little renown?

There are pleasures but not peace in the city.
There are pleasures but not peace in the town.
There is loneliness, despair and futility
Superficial celebrations cannot drown.
Where is the Prince of Peace of Christmas,
Son of God of so little renown?

Why is there fear in the streets of the city?
Why is there fear in the streets of the town?
Why are human hearts hard – without pity?
Why is the nation in sin tumbling down?
Is it because the Jesus of Christmas,
The Son of God, is of little renown?

Jesus came to save the sinner in the city.
Jesus came to save the sinner in the town.
He died on the cross for our iniquity.
For all sinners His life He laid down.
Where is the Jesus of Christmas?
He is risen! Savior! Lord of renown!

There is hope for the sinner in the city.
There is hope for the sinner in the town.
For the one who repents in sincerity
To follow the King God has crowned.
Where is the Jesus of Christmas?
On His throne, sovereign Lord of renown.

Praise the King of Kings of the city.
Praise the Lord of Lords of the town.
His reign endures through eternity.
Through Him alone salvation is found.
Who is the Jesus of Christmas?
He's either your Judge or your Lord of renown.

Then the angel said to them, "Do not be afraid, for behold, I bring you good tidings of great joy which will be to all people. For there is born to you this day in the city of David a Savior, who is Christ the Lord. Luke 2:10-11

... suddenly a voice came out of the cloud, saying, "This is My beloved Son, in whom I am well pleased. Hear Him!" Matthew 17:5

Infinite

$\mathcal{I}$nfinite the host of twinkling stars
Suspended in space as Jesus slumbered.
Amazing that the One Who created them
Had each star named and numbered.

Infinite the days since earth's creation
That men for Messiah had longed and waited.
In fullness of time by the wisdom of God
The first Christmas night was sovereignly dated.

Infinite the sufferings, sadness and sorrows
Jesus later at Calvary would bear.
Infinite, too, the mercies of God
Who for sinners placed Him there.

Infinite the lost on life's weary path
When Jesus' light to the dark world came.
Some chose Him as Savior, some chose God's wrath.
Still today but two choices remain.

Infinite today the myriads of souls
Dwelling in miry, deep pits of sin.
Jesus died on the cross to heal and make whole
He came to offer them peace from within.

Infinite the souls who by grace He would save
From every sinful generation.
Those who would receive Him as Savior and Lord
From every age and race and nation.

Infinite the eternity that fast encroaches
Upon the calendar of life's brief span.
None knows the day when for him it approaches.
One hope is offered: <u>one</u> salvation plan.

Infinite the significance of that wondrous night.
Infinite the gift, Son of God, King of Kings.
Infinite His rule – He'll return in power and might.
Infinite the blessings salvation freely brings.

Infinite the realms of time and space
Awaiting each trusting, repentant mortal.
Jesus' own presence, His love, mercy and grace,
And joy eternal beyond heaven's portals.

Infinite, infinite all human destiny.
The soul in heaven or hell will reside.
The Scriptures declare it for all to see.
God's Word is truth and will ever abide.

Infinite to infinity. But infinity where?
Life's most compelling question dare not be ignored.
The time is now to repent, to prepare!
To receive this Christmas the gift of the Lord.

*"... as many as received Him, to them He gave
the right to become children of God..."*
John 1:12

Heaven

My Home Is In Glory

My home is in glory.
My home is afar.
Its dwelling more distant
Than the furthermost star.

My home is in glory.
Its gates open and pearled.
And a divine deed awaiting
Since prior to the world.

My home is in glory.
Eternal its place.
Purchased by Jesus,
And offered by grace.

A home beckons in glory.
Or have you not heard?
God's promise, the truth
Of His wonderful Word?

My home is in glory.
Unsurpassed is its worth.
By faith I've surrendered
To Jesus on earth.

→

My home here is temporal.
It will soon pass away.
But Jesus will bring me
To His home one day.

And His home is in glory;
I trust and I know.
There's none that can offer
What He will bestow.

My home is in glory.
My home is secured
Through Jesus' atonement,
The death He endured.

My home is in glory.
He died for my sins.
Now I have repented.
I am living for Him!

My home is in glory,
By Jesus prepared.
In His resurrection
He desires all to be there.

No home is in glory---
How tragic it is!
For those who deny Him
The Lordship that's His.

My home is in glory.
What love, Oh what peace!
My home is with Jesus
Where joy will not cease.

Oh, there's a home in glory
All sinners can afford.
The key to it: repentance
And receiving Christ as Lord.

"Therefore, having been justified by faith, we have peace with God through our Lord Jesus Christ, through whom also we have access by faith into this grace in which we stand, and rejoice in hope of the glory of God." Romans 5:1-3

Why Should I?

Headed for heaven,
No small delight.
Why should I allow
Sad thoughts in the night?

Headed for heaven,
No small blessing.
Why should I allow
Satan's oppressing?

Headed for heaven,
No small place.
Why allow allegiance
To this temporal place?

Headed for heaven,
No small joy.
Why should I allow
Worry to annoy?

Headed for heaven,
No small welcome awaits.
Why should I allow
My praise to abate?

*"For he waited for the city which has foundations,
whose builder and maker is God."* *Hebrews 11:10*

View from Mount Nebo

*M*oses, God's beloved and ancient prophet,
In accordance with God's sovereign plan,
Was not permitted to cross the Jordan
To enter the Promised Land.

God did allow His servant Moses,
Before his journey on earth was done,
To ascend the craggy peak of Mount Nebo
For a glimpse of the land stretching far in the sun.

Moses then died with no earthly fortune.
He was quietly buried with no monument grand.
But he left a legacy of faithful service.
In his future was a glorious Promised Land.

Lord, keep me faithful as was faithful Moses
As I gaze from afar, as on earth I stand,
At the wonder and beauty of heaven's glory,
As I survey through Your Word that Promised Land.

They stretch to infinity, those golden acres.
My soul so yearns their full beauty to see.
From my distant peak here upon my Mount Nebo,
I peer enthralled at the land You have promised to me.

Deuteronomy Chapter 28

A Bit of Earth in Heaven?

If we could enjoy
One earthly bliss
In heaven,
Heaven would not
More heavenly be.
But, logically,
It seems to me,
That riding a bike
On heaven's lanes,
Joyful and free,
Just might be gain.
An earthly delight
Made more
Heavenly.
Pedaling,
Praising the Lord
For all heaven's sights,
With infinite glories
To see.

Looking Down

*T*hey called it a supermoon.
It tended
To look
As if it descended
To but a few miles
Above the earth.
An amazing sight
Of remembrance worth.
The next supermoon
Is years away,
And I cannot stay
Upon the ground
To gaze again upon it —
So enormously round!
I wonder if
It will seem
Insignificant and small
Or whether I'll notice it
At all
When I gaze upon it,
Looking not up
But down.
How different
Will be
All that I see
From heaven's view!
When earth and heaven
Are all made new.

Revelation Chapter 22

Upward Bound

*T*oday I watched a doe go bounding
Across a wide field into the trees.
How lithe and lovely were her motions.
Designed by divine choreography.

She leapt with grace and wild abandon.
Her hooves flew high as she soared free.
No other creature of the woodland
Endowed with such choreography.

Observing her brought me thrill and joy.
What a privilege it was to see
Her perform her delightful woodland ballet
By God's unique choreography.

One day my soul will bound toward heaven.
Leap in perfect peace and liberty.
Upward! Free as that doe bounding over the snow
By God's delightful, divine choreography.

Our Loss, Our Gain

*A*ge, among many other things,
Is a time of loss, a time of losing.
We have less and less choice
Over what years may bring,
Less power to do our own choosing.
We lose our loved ones.
We lose our stability.
We lose our strength
And cherished abilities.
We accomplish less
And we struggle each day,
We must confess,
With forgetfulness.
Still, age cannot
Be counted all loss
If we belong to Jesus the Lord.
There's more joy now
In the knowing
That homeward we're going
And all,
All is gain
Where we're headed toward.

"... absent from the body ...
present with the Lord."
2 Corinthians 5:8

Glimpses of Gold

There is no such time,
No matter what some may say,
In song or in rhyme,
As the golden years.
There is no gold in tears
Or in the inevitable fears
Of a new unknown.
Growing old is a stage
Never explored before.
Without compass, map
Or a single page
From life's former lore.
Golden? "No!" say those
Who decry
The term with scorn.
Who mourn
Their losses
As the years go by.
Until, at last,
They die.
But, in Christ ---
In Christ are
Golden glimpses,
Golden nuggets found.
Glimpses only for
The heaven-bound.

Glimpses of walking
Heaven's lanes.
Glimpses of no more
Of sin's dark stains.
Of no more sorrow
And no more pain.
All, all in eternity's
Wondrous gain.
Promise of eternal day.
Promise of no more night.
Glimpses of future glory
Shining ever bright.
God's glimpses
Of gold
Are His promises,
More precious as
We grow old.
All fulfilled
When Him
We behold.

*"... by which (the knowledge of Jesus) have
been given to us exceedingly great
and precious promises..."
2 Peter 1:4*

Revelation Chapter 21

Creation's Anxious Longing

*W*hen days are last in number
And the darkness sore abounds,
God's grace yet more abundant
Flows through love's atoning wounds.
　　But there's moaning
　　And there's groaning
For that glorious final call.
All creation yearns for freedom
That His presence brings us all.

Oh, it's with such anxious longing
That within ourselves we groan.
Aghast at sin surrounding
We grieve, but not alone.
　　For there's pleading,
　　Interceding,
By the Spirit---always heard!
And God gives hope victorious
In groanings far too deep for words.

There's groaning in our sorrows
And there's groaning in the test
For that glorious victory meeting
When the sons of God are blessed.
　　But there's praising
　　In our raising.
Soon He'll liberate the sphere
At the jubilant reunion
When that trumpet sound we hear!

Romans Chapter 8

Come, Lord Jesus

*E*ven so,
Come, Lord Jesus
Come!
Break through this darkness
Even as the sun
Breaks through the clouds
On storm-darkened day.
Come!
Even as the moon
Breaks through the night
To shine full and bright.
Come!
Come soon!
Be it during night
Or during day.
We fervently pray,
Lord, come!
Do not delay.

"Amen. Even so, come, Lord Jesus!"
Revelation 22:20

68216196R00086

Made in the USA
Lexington, KY
04 October 2017